D1123487

Orphans from the Sea

Orphans
from the Sea

words by Jack Denton Scott

photographs by
Ozzie Sweet

G.P. Putnam's Sons • New York

Text copyright © 1982 by Jack Denton Scott.
Photographs copyright © 1982 by Ozzie Sweet.
All rights reserved. Published simultaneously in
Canada by General Publishing Co. Limited, Toronto.
Printed in the United States of America.
Book design by Charlotte Staub.
Library of Congress Cataloging in Publication Data
Scott, Jack Denton,
Orphans from the sea.
Summary: Describes the work of the Suncoast Sanctuary,
which specializes in the rescue and repair of orphaned
and injured seabirds and other wild creatures.
1. Suncoast Seabird Sanctuary (Fla.)—Juvenile literature.
[1. Suncoast Seabird Sanctuary (Fla.) 2. Seabirds. 3. Wildlife rescue.
4. Bird refuges. 5. Birds—Florida] I. Sweet, Ozzie, ill. II. Title
QL676.5.S36   639.9'7829759'65   82-409   AACR2
ISBN 0-399-20858-5
First impression.

This is for our
friend and editor, Margaret Frith,
with appreciation for her guidance, enthusiasm
and encouragement—editorial talents
that are rare indeed.

JDS / OS

On a clear, sunny Florida day over the Gulf of Mexico, the large bird swooping low over that sea to look for a fish would have been flying much higher above the water. But today the sky was getting dark as storm clouds gathered on the horizon, and it was hard for him to see. The water was choppy and waves were building.

The bird was a mature American Bald Eagle and he was hungry. No longer a brown juvenile, he had recently acquired his magnificent white head feathers, the most familiar feature of our national bird. With a wingspread of 6½ feet, and eyesight that could spot his prey from as high up as 3 miles, he could soar for hours on the warm afternoon air currents, looking for prey.

But, suddenly, out of the black clouds on the horizon, winds raced in, growing stronger as they neared land. Called the *Nortes del huesco colorado*, or *chocolateros*, these northerly winds travel with such speed and strength that even a sturdy flyer like the eagle is helpless in their path.

As the wind caught up to the bird, it hurled him shoreward. So fierce was its force that the eagle could not control the direction of his flight and could only go where the wind drove him.

Over land now, the eagle was prevented by the storm clouds from seeing the stretch of power lines directly in his line of flight. Pushed by the wind, he hit the lines with such force that both wings received multiple fractures so severe that he would never fly again. But he would live—with help.

A black-headed Laughing Gull caught by the storm was luckier. It was flung against the hood of an automobile and injured, but with help it would fly again.

A large Brown Pelican with a 10-foot wingspread was smashed into a tree, shattering its long upper bill. It would die of starvation if it did not get the help it needed to survive.

Great Blue Herons

Storms are not the only cause of injuries to birds, although birds of all kinds are found in distress after a severe storm. Other acts of nature and people are responsible for creating many helpless animal orphans.

A pair of spiky-headed young Great Blue Herons were discovered in a nest, starving because their parents were caught in tangled fishing line and couldn't get back to feed them. An immature Green Heron was found floundering and hurt in a sea marsh. One orphaned pelican was born with a deformed upper bill, so that, without its parents or someone to feed it, it would starve. Another pelican, trailing fishing line, was trapped in a tree. It had gone after an artificial fishing lure, mistaking it for a fish. A majestic Red-tailed Hawk was shot by a hunter and left to die.

All of these injured birds would survive because medical help, nursing, protection, shelter and food were available at the Suncoast Seabird Sanctuary and they were lucky enough to be rescued.

Green Heron

The sanctuary grew out of a single incident that took place on a dark December afternoon in 1971 near Indian Shores on the west coast of Florida not far from St. Petersburg. Twenty-five-year-old Ralph Heath, Jr., was driving along the winding road beside the Gulf of Mexico when he saw a crippled bird on the beach. It was dragging a broken wing. The young man caught the bird, a cormorant, and took it to a veterinarian who pinned its wing and told Heath that the bird would need two months to recuperate. So Heath took the cormorant home to his father, a retired doctor, and his understanding mother.

He put the cormorant in a cardboard box in the recreation room of his parents' beachside home. Then he went off to the Redington Long Pier for some fish to feed the bird. He explained what he was doing to a sympathetic bait-shop owner who gave him some fish and the promise of more. Two days later, the man phoned to say that he had more fish and an injured Herring Gull he had found under the pier. The next day another fish supplier called saying he had just found a pelican tangled in fishing line. Heath picked up the bird, untangled it, found it was injured and took it home. Now he had three "patients" in the recreation room and more were to come.

Early one morning the Heaths found a cardboard box on their doorstep with a note taped to the top. *Bird inside, please help.* It was a Mourning Dove with a broken wing.

A local newspaper ran an article about the Good Samaritan to the birds, and before long Heath had to build recuperation pens outside on the beach to accommodate the growing number of birds brought to him.

He began to form the underlying philosophy of what would become his full-time occupation: the rescue, repair, recuperation and, whenever possible, the release of these birds.

But it would take more than the dedication of one person to build a working sanctuary for sick, deformed, abandoned and injured wild creatures. It would take the commitment of many to make it happen.

Fortunately, the idea of a sanctuary for wild creatures attracted the right people, and today the nationally famous Suncoast Seabird Sanctuary thrives, thanks to a lot of hard-working and dedicated staff members and volunteers. The sanctuary has grown but its original aims remain the same: Rescue, Repair, Recuperation and Release.

Rescue

A more complete description would be search and rescue, because the sanctuary doesn't wait for people to bring birds to them. They look for injured and orphaned birds in trouble and they find them everywhere: under fishing piers, near the beaches and out in the Gulf.

The staff members search the sea from an observation platform where they can also keep an eye on bird activity within the sanctuary itself. And they cruise the Gulf in a jet boat specially designed for high-speed maneuvering in shallow water.

They check under piers and in water close to the shoreline, where they are apt to find a pelican with fishing line wrapped around its bill. They tempt it with a fish so that they can get close enough to catch it. Then they cut the line and examine the bird carefully. If the bird is unharmed, they release it right away; but if it needs medical attention, they take it back to the sanctuary.

Cormorants

After patrolling the beaches, the boat heads out to deeper water, where they might see a collection of cormorants sunning themselves or a flock of pelicans. When they find a bird that can barely swim or fly, they coast in and catch it.

Pelicans

Other areas filled with seabirds, some of which might be in trouble, are the small islands of mangrove trees that grow on the muddy banks of estuaries. These thickly grown islands spotted along the west coast of Florida are rarely visited by people. They make ideal rookeries for Brown Pelicans and other birds. The birds return to the islands after fishing to nest for the night or to feed their young. Too often birds return trailing monofilament fishing line that gets tangled in the trees, trapping the birds to starve.

Red-tailed Hawk

As the sanctuary became widely known, more and more people began to bring birds and other animals directly to the staff for help. Newspapers, magazines, radio and television carried stories all over the country, and people everywhere got involved in their own rescue missions.

Three teenage boys drove 500 miles round trip from Miami Beach with an injured pigeon. A man from Texas, driving a pickup truck at night, hit a Barred Owl that flipped up into the back of the truck. The bird had been swooping down to capture a rat scurrying across the highway. Driving all night, the Texan delivered the owl to the sanctuary. Another Texan on his way back from Mexico found a small Screech Owl that had been hit by a car and left by the road.

Four sky divers jumping onto a beach on Florida's east coast found two abandoned baby terns. They borrowed a plane, landed near St. Petersburg and hitched a ride to bring the baby birds to the sanctuary. In North Carolina, a woman came across an injured tern on the beach. She chartered a twin-engined plane and two pilots at a cost of $3,000 to fly her and the bird to Florida.

Two men brought in a gull with a broken wing and a missing leg. They told an incredible story. A cat had chased the gull with its broken wing across a railroad track in front of an oncoming train. The train's wheel severed the gull's leg cleanly, exactly at the body line, crimping the flesh so that there was no bleeding. Marveling that the bird had managed to survive the broken wing, the cat and the train, the men rushed the gull to the sanctuary, where it survived.

A family cut their vacation short at faraway Key West to deliver a sandpiper with a broken wing, and two teenagers brought in a hawk that was almost killed when it attacked a large Yellow Rat Snake. The hawk had flown down and successfully grasped the snake in its claws. But before the snake died, it wrapped itself around the bird and contracted its muscles. The snake had to be cut away from the nearly dead hawk.

On an average day fifteen "rescued" birds are brought into the hospital, but as many as ninety-three have shown up in one day.

Blind pelican with his mate

Pelican with deformed upper bill

Repair

The first step back to health is rescue, but the second, repair, is what the Suncoast Seabird Sanctuary is all about. Could the injured be medically treated and then successfully returned to the wild? Many could, but some could not.

The resident population of the sanctuary stays at about 500 wild creatures. Two-thirds of these are permanently crippled and will remain there for the rest of their lives.

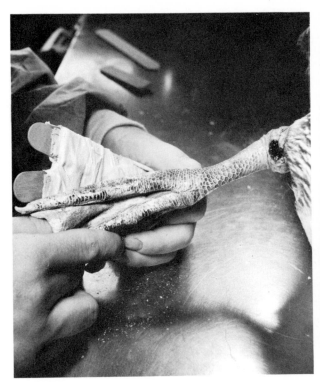

Injuries and afflictions are as varied as the species that arrive daily: ducks soaked and helpless from an oil spill; a Blue Jay severely injured by a cat; an egret that flew into a window; a Blue Heron sick from badly polluted water; a baby Great Horned Owl that had fallen from its nest, breaking a wing and a leg; three Wood Storks with broken wings; a pelican blinded from being beaten over the head with an oar; an American Bittern with a broken wing; a Red-tailed Hawk blinded by bird shot; a Great Horned Owl permanently crippled from flying into a microwave tower; a buzzard hit by a car.

From the beginning, the staff at the sanctuary—although they always consulted veterinarians—attempted some of the repair themselves. And their ingenuity worked. A pelican with a shattered upper bill was given a new one made from plastic construction pipe; a Great Egret with a leg broken by an automobile had its leg amputated and was fitted with a peg leg made from a wooden bird perch, tongue depressors and tape. Both of these birds were able to function with these "repairs."

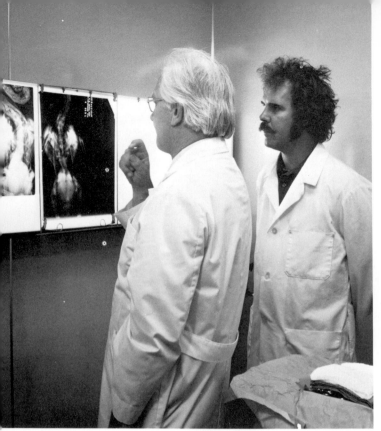
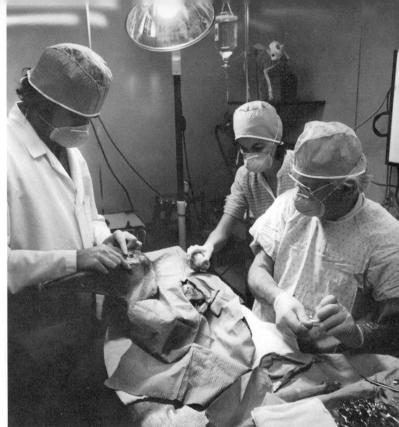

Today there are six full-time employees led by Ralph Heath, Jr. The others are Dianna King, Outdoor Rehabilitation Supervisor, and her assistant, Connie Plisko; Sandi Middleton-Smith, Operations Manager; and two Veterinarian Technicians, Allen Foley and Karl Almquist, who have taken the Junior College Veterinarian Program, which equips them to handle minor injuries and repairs. They have taught the rest of the staff to assist them in repair work. Weekend volunteers bring the staff to about a dozen. Heath's mother runs the office and his father is the genial gatekeeper.

Sandi Middleton-Smith often assists Technician Karl Almquist in removing fishhooks from birds, as does Veterinarian Technician Volunteer Cindy Shirley. The hooks and hook damage are everywhere, eyes, skin, legs, heads, bills, necks and the inside of mouths. After birds are treated and before they are placed in enclosures for observation and further care, they are number-banded with a metal band on the leg. The

26

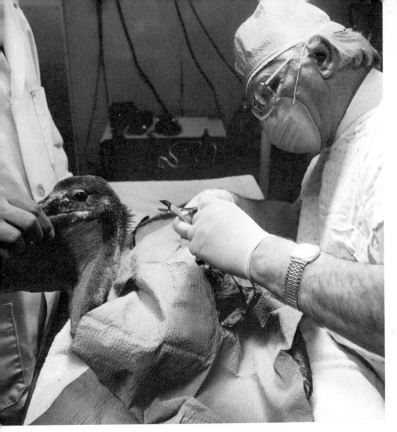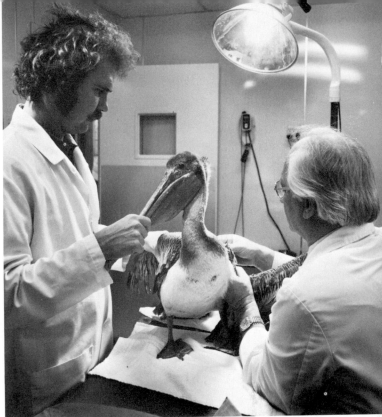

number is entered into the admissions-and-records book for identification and case-history purposes.

But medical care involves much more than repair and records. A medical technician continually makes extensive microscopic analyses of blood and fecal samples. This diagnostic activity is an important ongoing part of the sanctuary's medical function, as technicians attempt to determine the causes of birds' illnesses. Force-feeding with vitamins, special foods and medications, and inoculations are also a part of medical treatment.

Serious injuries or illnesses are always handled by doctors of veterinary medicine. Dr. Harold F. Albers is a favorite of both birds and staff. So concerned and adept is this doctor that he has perfected a most delicate and complicated operation for repairing tears in a pelican's fleshy pouch. He also has successfully constructed an artificial bill for a pelican and virtually rebuilt a foot.

Why do Brown Pelicans greatly outnumber other birds at the sanctuary? Unfortunately, people who fish and the fact that pelicans themselves are such able, alert fishers, are responsible. Fish is the pelican's natural, preferred food and it will even go after artificial lures and live bait. Eighty-five percent of the injuries to pelicans treated at the sanctuary are from hooks and monofilament fishing lines.

From treating hundreds of birds with fishhook injuries, the sanctuary workers have learned that even the smallest injury may have serious consequences. Some relatively minor injuries have left birds permanently crippled, and without proper care they would die. Fishhooks tear flesh and cause infections. Fishing lines can wrap around a bird's leg or wing and cut off the supply of blood, causing the eventual loss of wing or leg. The strong lines can also trap birds in trees, either strangling them or tangling them in branches until they die of starvation.

The Suncoast Seabird Sanctuary staff offers this advice for handling a bird in trouble. First, be cautious: Always get someone to help in handling a hooked bird. It is almost impossible to hold a bird and work on it successfully without assistance. Second, be careful: All seabirds will try to protect themselves by striking at your face or eyes with their long, sharp bills. Try to cover the bird's head with a towel, shirt or blanket. Most birds are quieter if they can't see.

When a bird is hooked on a fishing line, gently and carefully reel in the hooked bird, trying to avoid breaking the line. If the bird escapes with a hook in it and part of the line trailing, the line may wrap around its bill or get tangled in a tree. The best method for getting the bird out of the water is with a hand net, if you are in a boat, or a large hoop net if you are on a pier or bridge.

Once the bird is captured, there are some steps to take if you feel capable. If not, try to get the hooked bird to a veterinarian. But don't just cut the fishing line and let the bird escape.

If the bird is just tangled in the line and not hooked, carefully remove *all* line. If a hook is in the skin below the bird's lower bill, and the barb is visible, hold the bill firmly and cut the barb off the hook and back the hook out. *Caution:* Cover the barb before cutting so that it can't fly off and injure you. If the barb of the hook is in the skin tissue just below the surface, push the barb forward until it is outside the skin; then cut off the barb and back the hook out.

The best advice of all concerns prevention. Before casting a fishing line, make certain no pelican or other seabird, which can dive for your bait or lure, is flying overhead. If you see one, wait until it leaves your vicinity before casting. Never fish close to any seabird on the water. Never leave baited fishing tackle out in the open unattended. Do not leave hooks or lures dangling from an exposed, unattended fishing rod. Do not throw old fishing line or other discards into the water. Do not feed seabirds in an area where anyone is fishing.

But injuries to pelicans are not all from fishing lines and hooks. The list of other mishaps is long and sometimes gory. One pelican was hit by a truck that tore off one wing completely and broke the other one in several places. Another pelican shattered its upper bill diving for a fish that someone had nailed to a board submerged in water. Both are alive and well as permanent "walking" residents of the sanctuary.

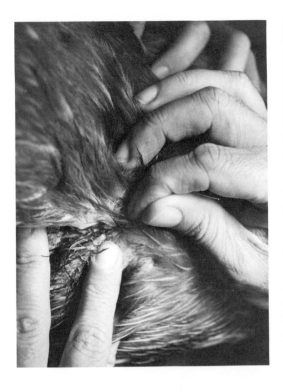
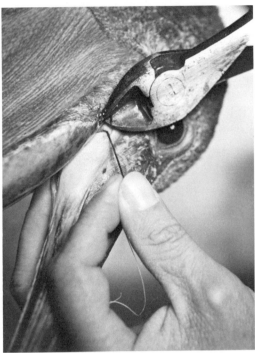
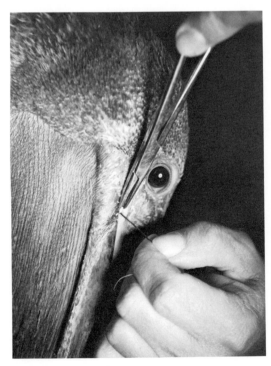
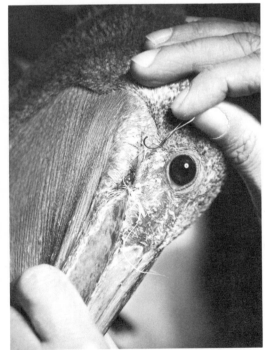

Pelicans are the stars of the compound because of their number and their appealing personalities. These long-billed, odd-looking creatures have survived from prehistoric times, but now they are high on the Endangered Species list in the United States because it is feared they will not make it into the next century.

Studies by biologists in states where the Brown Pelican was once numerous and is now scarce have proved that DDT, DDE, and polychlorinated biphenyls—PCBs or plasticides—were responsible for its decline. Brown Pelicans developed high concentrations of these chemicals in their bodies from eating fish in chemically polluted waters. Pelicans were laying eggs with shells too thin to support the weight of the adult nesting birds, and the shells cracked before the babies could hatch. The pelican population suffered a drastic decline in Texas, South Carolina and California and it had completely vanished in Louisiana, where pelicans had once been so numerous that it was named the state bird.

But with the banning or regulation of the use of chemicals there has been a turn for the better. Breeding birds have been taken to Louisiana from Florida and the results have given us reason for cautious optimism. Yet in California and South Carolina, where huge populations of Brown Pelicans once thrived, their numbers are down to about 3,000 in each state and Texas has fewer than 100.

Pelicans

One place, however, where everybody must be doing something right is the Suncoast Seabird Sanctuary. Their success in breeding disabled birds that produce healthy chicks, which can then be released in the wild or taken to areas where pelicans are being reintroduced, has amazed bird experts everywhere.

The fact that most of the permanent-resident birds are crippled and only have one wing or one leg doesn't deter them from pairing up and building nests from sticks and other nesting material provided by the staff. There is nothing genetically wrong with these birds and to date they have produced 130 sound, healthy baby Brown Pelicans that have been released to join wild flocks in Florida.

Wild pelicans, free-flyers—or "freeloaders," as the staff calls them—also fly in to mate with the crippled birds. And while outsiders praise the sanctuary's success with breeding pelicans in captivity, the staff doesn't consider it unusual. They credit their success to providing the birds with good living conditions and a constant supply of food.

Because the pelicans in the sanctuary receive a year-round food supply, they nest twice a year, in summer and in winter. Pelicans living in the wild have to struggle to survive in winter and only nest in the summer. During the winter months in Florida, harsh, strong winds drive the surface, or bait, fish far out into deep water. This places the pelicans in a desperate situation, for these fish are their normal food supply. But the wild, free-flying birds are aided in their struggle for survival by the sanctuary.

During the winter months, hundreds of these wild pelicans "move in." On a normal feeding day in summer about 350 pounds of fish are eaten in one feeding by the residents. But in winter, when free-flying pelicans and other seabirds come in to feed, as much as 800 pounds of fish are consumed. But even in winter, if the weather is good, the wild birds prefer to return to the sea and seek their own food naturally.

As the birds feed, they are carefully observed and if any of them appear listless or weak and uninterested in eating, they are taken to the Emergency Room for observation and, if necessary, treatment.

Fish, mainly Spanish Sardines and Thread Herring, costs $15,000 a year. Other kinds of food are needed too: high-protein dog food, sometimes as much as 600 pounds a month; 200 pounds of ordinary bird feed—sunflower seeds, etc.—a month; and about 160 pounds of horse-meat a month for raptors—hawks and owls.

Donations from industry and individuals supply the $50,000 needed each year, but the costs mount steadily. With great skill, Heath keeps his mission in public view in magazines, on radio and television, and by giving lectures, which bring in donations and memberships. But the need is constant.

Recuperation

Diligent feeding and careful observation accomplish the third aim of the Suncoast Seabird Sanctuary—recuperation.

Nursing the sick, the injured and the mistreated back to health and, when possible, freedom, is done gently and generously by the staff and

volunteers. The feathered residents even have their own bathing tubs, filled with fresh water that is changed frequently. As fresh water is poured into the tubs, the birds race to be first in.

Birds of a feather, so to speak, are kept together. For example, in Pen One, all the birds have been together for seven years. There are seven pairs, plus two pairs of free-flyers that seem to have decided this is the good life and stay on. When possible, birds of the same age, or with a similar affliction and strength level, are kept together.

The personal touch is all important. The pelican that was blinded after being struck on the head with an oar is named Big Blind Pelican and comes when he is called. There are a number of blind birds at the sanctuary, which must be hand-fed. They have adapted to one location and they move about confidently in that area. They are so attuned to the sounds of feeding time that they run to meet whoever is bringing in their food with mouths open to receive it.

Mush Mouth, the pelican with the deformed upper bill, also needs to be hand-fed, and he runs to Dianna King and nudges her when he is hungry.

The eagle that flew into the power lines needed considerable medical attention and long nursing. In fact, when he first arrived he was in such bad condition that it was almost certain he wouldn't survive. But each day he got stronger and his appetite improved. In spite of the severe wing damage, he can balance on a perch and he is beginning to grow new feathers. He will never fly again, but he will never have to hunt for his food and fight the elements for survival.

Ned, the adult Sandhill Crane, likes to stroll with Dianna King, and only Dianna. Ned, physically perfect, was dropped off at the sanctuary

by a stranger. The bird screams every time he sees small boys, which suggests that he was raised illegally from a young bird and perhaps mistreated by children. Ned is too tame to be released, and he is prized for his mouse-catching abilities.

Sundance, a Barred Owl, both wings permanently crippled when he was shot by a hunter, was found by a rancher and brought in for help. He is "manned" by Sandi Middleton-Smith and responds to her alone. She exercises him and feeds him frozen chicks daily.

Some birds will exercise voluntarily, pelicans especially. But hawks and owls must be encouraged. They are tethered by lines or jesses, which are gradually lengthened as the birds become accustomed to the daily wing-flapping routine they must do.

The hawks and owls point up the fact that, even though this remarkable "hospital" is built only a few feet from the Gulf of Mexico, not all of its residents are seabirds or even shorebirds.

Yet the list of orphans from the sea is long, for the sanctuary's 53 species include a wide range: Double-crested Cormorants, Gannets, Great Egrets, Snowy Egrets, Great Blue Herons, Yellow-crowned Night Herons, Anhingas, four species of gulls (Herring, Ring-billed, Laughing and Bonaparte's), Royal Sandwich Terns, Red Knot Sandpipers, Ruddy Turnstone Sandpipers. But no wild creature is ever turned away. Fish Crows, Mourning Doves, Blue Jays, Red-winged Blackbirds, Starlings, hawks, owls, vultures, even snakes and turtles have been helped.

So varied and interesting is the wildlife at the Suncoast Seabird Sanctuary that the staff decided to open its gates to the public, free of charge. If they could show people the work they were doing as it was being done, they could help everyone understand and care about wild creatures.

For example, Dianna King conducts tours for school children and civic groups. To drive home and dramatically illustrate her point about protecting and respecting wildlife, she brings out Jezebel, a magnificent, physically perfect-looking Red-tailed Hawk. She is perfect, except that she is blind. Shot in the head by a hunter and left to die, she has three pellets lodged so close to the brain that to remove them would kill her.

With Jezebel fluttering on her gloved hand, Dianna tells the children about the cruel act that caused the bird to be brought to the sanctuary, and how the hawk actually helps us all by killing rodents, which eat our crops. She points out the bird's beauty and she tells a story that shows how sensitive wild creatures are.

Once a volunteer was helping to hold the hawk down while jesses were fastened to her legs. The holding, which was a little rough because the volunteer was unskilled, lasted for five mintues, with Jezebel resisting fiercely. Four years later, the usually docile blind hawk began screaming wildly at a man outside her aviary. The man was bearded and Dianna didn't recognize him at first. But Jezebel knew him right away. He was the volunteer who had held her so roughly four years before, and she must have recognized his voice.

Sandi Middleton-Smith also conducts tours, guiding the public through the sanctuary, pointing out what has happened to the birds, showing graphic evidence of the good and the bad that people can do. She talks about the needs and the aims of the sanctuary. She explains that anyone can "adopt" a bird for a small monthly fee that will pay for its feed. She tells about the actor Pat O'Brien who, when visiting one day, adopted a pelican. A new patient was brought in, a young Brown Pelican with a fishhook in its eye and a damaged wing. Pat O'Brien immediately adopted it and has continued to be an enthusiastic supporter of the sanctuary, financially and vocally. Sandi also confides that Pelican Pat is now a grandfather.

Sandi gets cheers when she tells about Pelican Pat appointing himself guardian to a wingless gull and helping it to its feet whenever it loses its balance and falls.

The dedication of the staff is obvious even to the casual visitor who comes just "to see the birds." The visitor is impressed and amazed at the care the patients receive at this hospital. One man said, "We don't have

people this concerned in our people hospitals!" And from America's most famous birdman, Roger Tory Peterson, comes the word, "Unbelievable," when he describes the work done at the sanctuary.

But it is the last of the four cornerstones of the foundation upon which the sanctuary was built that is the ultimate, if sometimes impossible, goal of everyone—release.

Release

The staff's and volunteers' most valuable reward after nursing a bird to health is watching it, carefully testing it, so that when it is finally released it will be physically fit to rejoin its own kind in the wild.

Although the list of permanent residents is long, it is encouraging and a tribute to the staff's skill and dedication that of every 20 birds treated only one must remain to live out its life as a cripple, while the other 19 fly to freedom.

Since its inception in 1971, the sanctuary has returned over 10,000 birds to the free world of flight. Additionally, some of their birds go to places such as Disney World's Pelican Bay; Sea World; Silver Springs; Busch, Cypress and Sunken Gardens.

So the functions of the Suncoast Seabird Sanctuary are many faceted: replenishing the vanishing pelican population; nursing wounded and sick birds back to health and returning them to their natural world; lecturing people on the importance of respecting and understanding wildlife; helping other facilities with wild birds; and providing a home for those that can't make it on their own in the wild.

Everyone at the sanctuary realizes that the only truly happy birds are those that are wild and free. They also know that, next to returning a bird to the wild, the most satisfying accomplishment in their own work is to see that the maimed, the crippled, the wingless, the one-legged, the blind and the deformed will be tenderly cared for, well fed and protected for as long as they live.

Lesser men and women caused the injuries that put a number of the birds in this unique hospital for wild creatures. Better men and women there atone for that cruelty and carelessness.

Also by
Jack Denton Scott and
Ozzie Sweet

Moose

The Book of the Pig

The Submarine Bird

The Book of the Goat

Island of Wild Horses

The Gulls of Smuttynose Island

Little Dogs of the Prairie

Return of the Buffalo

Canada Geese

That Wonderful Pelican

Loggerhead Turtle

City of Birds and Beasts

Window on the Wild
by Jack Denton Scott
illustrated by Geri Greinke